TRUTH TOLD IN COVID TIMES

2020 – THE YEAR WE MADE IT THROUGH THE CRISIS

By Sarah Chaplin

ISBN: 978-1-8381143-1-2

First Edition: August 2020

The cover photograph shows a dandelion seed head. After the flower forms, then comes the seed, and on average over two hundred seeds on each stem. When the seeds are dispersed they land, and germinate.

My prayer is that these nuggets of truth be like seeds that find their way to your heart, wherever you are, and land there.

Truth sets us free, in the words of Jesus. Truth changes our lives for the better, and this is the essence of Truth Told.

Photo by Ante Hamermit on Unsplash

INTRODUCTION

The clock struck midnight and we welcomed in the New Year. 2020 was about to dawn, and how little did we know what the coming months would hold for us all, and how our world would be turned upside down.

We all started off in January by recovering from a busy December and maybe setting out our goals for the year, updating our newly purchased diary, and endeavouring to lose those added pounds that had crept up unawares over the Christmas season. The diary has spent most of the time gathering dust on our shelves, as life, as we know life, began to take a different twist.

We got through February, longing for the springtime, and then, with the hope of things getting brighter and more vibrant with nature coming alive. We hit March and the Covid-19 virus came to our attention, and as much as we hoped it would be contained in China, this was never the case.

We celebrated Mothers Day in the UK on Sunday 22nd March, and as a family we had a roast lunch with close friends of ours. It really felt rather like the Last Supper, because by the morning we would be on official lockdown. That was Monday 23rd March 2020, and everything changed.

A war-time atmosphere filled the air, where we were almost waiting for air raid sirens. Within days the shops ran out of flour. It was reminiscent of the stories of the old days where families were on rations.

For key workers, life would need to continue, and essential services would need to be provided, particularly in the caring profession and food supplies.

I continued in my job as hospital chaplain, though we knew some drastic changes were required in our department and we would face challenges in the hospital.

It was during lockdown that *Truth Told* was born. This is how it happened. On Sunday 8th March, my husband Glen and I were preaching in our friends' church in Ammanford, South Wales. At the end of the service, the pastor, who is a close friend of ours, came up to me and said, 'It begins today.' I wasn't quite sure what that meant at first, although something in my heart did a huge leap. I had a feeling that this was the time for a dream to come true.

All my adult life I have loved communicating truth. I have passionately done so in many different settings, in hundreds of locations. From school assemblies, the workplace, conferences, church services and other groups who request an after-dinner speaker. I had never thought of doing it any other way other than face to face.

Over lunch with the friends, our colleague said that I needed a website with which to communicate truth. This would be a digital platform for bringing inspirational messages that had the potential to change people's lives. He said that all the costs for this venture were already taken care of and the website designer, was on standby to get the site built with the content I would provide, and we would get that finalised over the following weeks.

TRUTH TOLD

I had tears streaming down my face. In that moment a dream was realised. It was happening.

We got home to Cornwall, and I slowly began gathering content and writing blogs and starting the process of getting Truth Told off the ground. I was balancing this with working part time as a chaplain in ever-changing circumstances.

Then, on the evening of Sunday 26th April, I was taken unwell at home, and the following morning it was confirmed that I had appendicitis. I had surgery that evening. Within twenty-four hours I was home from hospital to recuperate. I needed some weeks off work to recover fully, and once I began to feel better, I sat quietly in our garden, reading, writing and planning, and all of a sudden, during my resting, the Truth Told vision developed even further. This enabled the *Truth Told* website to be launched on Monday 1st June 2020, along with the Facebook page with video blogs.

Truth Told seemed to have come at the right time for me personally, and at an opportune time to bring encouragement to others. I decided to regularly produce some short video clips, with inspiring messages from the heart, to lift our spirits and share nuggets of truth – the sort of truth that changes us for the better, truth that sets us free, as Jesus says in John chapter 8.

So, in this small book I have brought together some transcripts from the Facebook page and blogs from the website, and as we reflect on them, maybe in some small way we will all realise they have helped us a little as we have taken this unusual journey through an international pandemic.

One day, we may have a young child climb up on our lap and they will say, 'Tell me about 2020 and the coronavirus,' and then we will recall how it all unfolded, and how we got through and what helped us.

You could then reach up to your bookshelf and say, 'Let me show you this little book. This is something that helped me and my friends at that time.' That's my hope, and that's my goal in collating these talks in this way.

19 small chapters for Covid-19 times!
Happy reading, and God bless you.

1

THE UNEXPECTED PLACE

Where should you have been? Maybe working in your office, in school about to sit examinations, on holiday in a sunny destination, running your business, or in the pattern of your usual daily routines, whatever they might be. You should have been in a different location with different people around you, and then Covid-19 took you to an 'unexpected place'.

We didn't plan to be here or make any arrangements that would help us prepare for this big relocation. We found ourselves where we never thought we would be, and where we didn't actually want to be.

If that was the case, then we are in good company with some characters in the Bible who experienced the same: Joseph, firstly in the pit and then the palace, Daniel in a den of lions, Jonah in the belly of a big fish, and Paul and Silas in jail—to name just a few.

When you find yourself in a place you never chose to be, remember that God loves you, sees you, and watches over you there. It can be a lonely place, a confusing place, and an isolating place, but a place where you can find God and see Him at work in your life. God often works in unexpected places in unexplained ways, and as the song says:

> 'Even when I can't see it You're working, You never stop, You never stop working...Way maker, miracle worker, promise keeper, Light in the darkness, my God, that is who You are. *

WE FOUND OURSELVES WHERE WE NEVER THOUGHT WE WOULD BE

If we can keep trusting in God and praising Him, despite being found in a strange place, we too will find God here. Proverbs 3:5 says, 'Trust in the Lord with all your heart and lean not on your own understanding.'

*'Way Maker' is a song originally released in 2016 by Sinach, and by Leeland , 2019.

The unexpected place

2

BEING AND DOING

About eight or nine years ago I learnt a big life lesson.

I drove home from work, filled the kettle to make my usual hot drink, and my wrist failed. I could do no more! I was born with one hand, and after doing all of the work for many years, it decided to give in. It needed a complete rest. I saw a consultant surgeon within two days, and he said that unless I did nothing for a month, he would need to operate. That thought frightened me, so I obeyed his instructions. I rested—couldn't do anything.

I began to think about how my worth and value was caught up with things that I did: my achievements, successes, the things that fulfil me, the things that I'm active with during my day. They are meaningful and important. They are me, aren't they?

I learnt, during that time, that being is much more important than doing. All our doing springs out of our being. I learnt this the hard way, I guess.

When Jesus was being baptised in the River Jordan by his

cousin John the Baptist, He heard these words from his Heavenly Father from heaven saying, 'This is my Son, whom I love; with him I am well pleased.' Matthew 3:17. That was before Jesus *did* anything. His value wasn't based on performance, nor God's love for Him on achievement.

Jesus hadn't done any miracles or raised anyone from the dead by then, or taught parables, or told stories, or interacted with people and changed their lives. He hadn't done that yet and still God says these words of affirmation to Him.

I think maybe there's a lesson there for all of us today: we are pleasing to God just by being who we are. Our being is more important than our doing.

At this time of Covid-19 crisis, when all of our doing may have changed and our daily lives may look very different to what they usually do, remember that our doing doesn't define our value. Things may have changed, but we are still the people God loves, so just remember that today. Maybe we need more being, and much less doing.

Maybe we need more being,

and much less doing.

3

HOLD TIGHT

'Cling to what is good...' Romans 12:9

'Hold on tight! Hold on tight!' That's my instruction to my children whenever they go on a ride at a funfair or something that is risky, regardless of how old they are. 'Just hold on tight.'

And if they should happen to drag me with them – note to self – 'Sarah...hold on tight, even if your knuckles are getting white. This ride will come to an end and we will all be OK...if we hold on tight.' I can hear myself. It's what you do as a parent, I guess, as you want to protect your family.

Look at the clematis plant in the picture, found in a section of our garden where I love to sit and catch the evening sun. It's incredible to see her holding on tight to the structure.

That's the important aspect of holding tight: you've got to know that what you are holding onto is strong enough to sustain you. And at these times of Covid-19 pandemic, or any other difficult times of life, for that matter, we need to be doing the same – holding on tight.

The Bible says we need to 'serve Him, hold fast to Him' Deuteronomy 10:20 simply because He is strong enough to carry us through. The book of Romans also says that we are to 'cling to everything that is good'. Chapter 12:9. We can try to hold tight to our finances, our business, our family, and our friends, and everyone who is in our world. We cling, and we hold on, but sometimes those things and those people can fail us, but when we cling onto God, who is our rock, He is able to sustain us, and able to hold us. We can cling to Him and He will bring us through.

So hold on tight. Be careful what you are holding on tight to. It needs to be able to sustain you.

WHAT YOU ARE HOLDING ON TO NEEDS TO BE STRONG ENOUGH TO SUSTAIN YOU

Hold tight

4

BEST AND WORST

"It was the best of times, it was the worst of times, it was the age of wisdom, it was the age of foolishness, it was the epoch of belief, it was the epoch of incredulity, it was the season of light, it was the season of darkness, it was the spring of hope, it was the winter of despair."

Charles Dickens - A Tale of Two Cities

This quotation so perfectly sums up the coronavirus pandemic of 2020. Crisis times certainly do have the potential for bringing out the best and the worst in society as a whole, and in us as individuals.

We have become aware of untold random acts of kindness in our communities; that's the best way to bless our communities.We have seen key-workers give of their absolute best in their care of others. We have been learning new recipes, enjoying the simple things of life, digging out that board game and reading that book that's been on our list. Those things have been the best times in our homes.

We have needed to think more creatively about how we communicate and keep in contact with each other. Mastering new technology; that's the best growth in our skills.

We are getting things finished that have been pending for too long. Completing anything on our 'to do' list is the best feeling.

Some of the worst results of this crisis are the financial struggles affecting many people, and there has been a sharp rise in the number of people needing to access food banks and emergency aid.

There is the possibility for frustration and despair as the situation takes its toll, and it brings out the worst in us.

For those who suffer with mental health issues, this time of loneliness and limited access to support has caused a big increase in depression, despair and even suicide. These issues are the worst sort, as they are invisible, but real.

There is the potential for being judgmental, impatient and selfish...just think 'toilet rolls'! The shelves were empty!

As Charles Dickens said, yes there is the experience of the 'winter of despair' but there is also a 'spring of hope.'

Sarah Chaplin

IN WHAT WAYS HAS COVID 19 TIMES BROUGHT OUT THE BEST AND WORST IN YOU?

5

WORRY

'Don't worry.' 'You worry too much.' 'Don't worry about it.' Do you ever say those things?

I think they are times when, if we are really honest, we have some additional worries. The international pandemic we are experiencing causes us to have some concerns. Not just about whether we might contract the virus ourselves and become unwell, but possibly financial concerns, family worries, anxiety for our children's wellbeing because they are not connecting with their friends in school and learning in the usual way.

We may have elderly parents and we had concerns for them, or family a long distance away and wondered when we might see them next.

We have a much-loved daughter and son-in-law living in

Canada and we were due to travel there for a visit in the spring of 2020, and that couldn't happen. So we wondered when we would see them next. When could we safely fly there? Is that a legitimate concern and worry as a parent? I think it's acceptable, and I give myself permission to say, 'Yes, that's a concern.'

In Matthew chapter 6, Jesus tells us not to worry. He tells us this because He wants to remind us that He can look after us and has made every provision for us. He encourages us not to worry, because worrying means we are trying to take things into our own hands instead of trusting Him. The minute we stop casting our cares upon Him and trying to work them all out for ourselves, that's when worry can set in.

Jesus goes on to say, in John's Gospel chapter 14, 'Do not let your hearts be troubled.' In other words, sometimes we do have worries and concerns, but Jesus says, 'Do not let that worry afflict you so much that you become troubled.' When your worry develops into something that causes you to lose peace of mind, sleep, appetite and concentration, when you feel disturbed by your worries, that's a difficult time, isn't it?

So Jesus says, 'Let me look after you. Put your trust in me and I will help you with your worries.' The old English original word for worry actually means 'to strangle', and I think worry has the capacity to strangle us and hold us in a vice and a tight grip.

So Jesus encourages us to try to worry less and to trust more. Don't worry about the things that you can't solve or fix at the moment. Embrace today and let Jesus take hold of tomorrow, because tomorrow has its own cares.

Not that we ever do worry, of course! But if we ever did, here are some helpful things for us to consider:

One day when Jesus was talking to disciples He said, 'In this world you will have trouble' (John 16:33). 'Great!' I would have thought to myself. 'Thanks for that! We thought that you would come to make everything good again.'

Jesus goes on to say, 'But take heart! I have overcome the world.' What this really means is that there isn't a problem that you and I go through that Jesus can't help us with, and bring us out the other side of.

DON'T BE AFRAID
BECAUSE I HAVE
OVERCOME THE WORLD

Someone once likened worry to a rocking chair: it gives you something to do but it doesn't get you anywhere. Have you ever noticed that worry is really distracting to our minds, causing us to be restless, and it doesn't actually solve any of our problems? Rather, sometimes it creates further ones.

Jesus gives us some sound advice about what we can do when we feel worried. If He affirms we're going to have troubles, and addresses the whole issue about worry in Matthew chapter 6, mentioning that word seven times, then He truly understands what we go through and can help us.

In the book of Philippians, Paul says that when we are anxious, we should present our requests to God in prayer, with thanksgiving, and then God's peace can flood our hearts.

I love to talk to a friend when I'm facing something that I'm worried about, and I'm sure you do too; someone who listens and cares, and who will come alongside me.

How much more wonderful is it when we talk to God about our worries! He is the one who created us, who knows us, and promises to never leave us nor forsake us. That is really good news, and it gives us comfort.

When worries and concerns come our way, when troubles come, we know exactly where we can turn. When the troubles come, as they often will, remember that Jesus will help us to overcome.

The One who created us, knows us,
and promises to never leave us.

6

KEEP RUNNING

In 2019, I achieved something I never thought would be possible. I have always enjoyed walking and the outdoors, but the big challenge for me was in running my first ever 5K race. It was Race for Life in Penzance, Cornwall, and I was running with eight friends from work, some who had previously run a 5k or 10k, and some a half-marathon, and then there was 'little old me', who had never run before.

I bought new running shoes, new kit, went to the gym for some training, lost a little bit of weight and began to get ready. The big day came, and as we stood at the starting line I had this thought: 'What have you let yourself in for?' We set off, and right from the start my colleagues were so incredible. They kept saying to me through the entire race, 'Come on, you can do this! Sarah, it's your first race and you are doing so well. Keep going! We're halfway now, and you're doing brilliantly!'

Well, I was hardly doing brilliantly, but their encouragement just kept me going. We got to the last one hundred metres and something beautiful happened. The two friends I was running with at that moment said, 'Now Sarah, run like the wind and get over that finishing line, ring the bell and get your medal. Go, girl! We're not coming with you. This is your moment!'

I ran like crazy and did exactly as they said. I crossed the finishing line and reached up and rang the bell and I got my reward, which I will always treasure. I ran the race with adrenalin and encouragement, and minimal skill, but it was the most amazing experience.

I want to be the sort of a person who encourages others to go forward, just like my friends did. The Apostle Paul says that life is like a race.

As he gets towards the end of his life, when speaking to Timothy he says, 'I have fought the good fight, I have finished the race, I have kept the faith. Now there is in store for me the crown of righteousness.' (2 Timothy 4: 7-8).

In the book of Galatians, also written by Paul, there's a verse that says, 'You were running a good race. Who cut in on you?' (Galatians 5:7). In other words, 'Who tried to knock you off course?' I do not want to be that person. I want to be the one who, like my colleagues, said, 'Go, girl!'

It's a challenge for us: do we encourage others, or cut in and hinder them? I know what sort of person I aspire to be and I'm sure so do you.

I have finished the race

7

DARKNESS

What is it about the dark that can sometimes make us feel afraid? It's because we can't see what is around us, and we can't see what is ahead. There's an element of uncertainty and the unknown.

Maybe there's something about this Covid-19 pandemic that has brought some darkness into this season of our lives; darkness into our heart, and darkness into our outlook. We can't see the light at the end of the tunnel, but I believe that that light is coming for all of us.

Just because we can't see things happening the way we do in the light, it doesn't mean God is not working. He is working in our darkness and He is working in the light. He's working in front of our faces, and He's working behind the scenes, but we know He is always working.

God does wonderful things in the darkness. Think of when a seed is planted in the soil in the garden. It is buried there underneath the darkness of the soil, and that's when beautiful things happen: germination. Things are bursting forth within that seed, and they come to light. They form a beautiful plant that gives you fruit or flowers (or both).

In the darkness miracles happen. Psalm 139 says that we were 'knitted together in our mother's womb', in a secluded place. In the mystery of that place, God was working there, knitting us and forming us. What a beautiful thing was happening in that dark place as you and I were being made!

WE MUSTN'T FEAR THE DARKNESS, BECAUSE GOD IS WORKING THERE

The first few verses of the Bible, Genesis chapter 1 verses 1-3, tell us that in the beginning God created the heavens and the earth. It says that at that time there was darkness, and that the Spirit of God was at work.

And then it says that God spoke into that darkness and said, 'Let there be light.' So there was darkness, but when God's Spirit, and then God's word and God's voice, came into the play, He brought light.

In the same way, any darkness that we might feel at the

minute could be actually setting the scene for God to do wonderful things and shine His light on the situation.

Could it be that in dark times, when we can't see clearly, God is working within us, germinating dreams, ideas, hopes, aspirations and things for our future? He's planting seeds in us that will produce fruit.

I pray that that's the case for you. I pray that God will shine His light on you, and through you, today. Psalm 18:28 says, 'For you light my lamp; The LORD my God illumines my darkness' (NASV). That's my prayer for you today.

8

LOSS

One thing is absolutely certain in life: we will experience loss at some point. Small losses, a big loss, or life-changing loss that will impact us hugely—loss will come our way.

Maybe it's the loss of relationship, of hope, of peace, of purpose, of identity, the loss of a job, or even the loss of the contents of your bank account if you have teenagers, as I have.

Loss takes many different forms, and all loss must be acknowledged, brought out into the light, and grieved over, so that we can find some healing from God and move forward.

During the Covid-19 crisis there has been an awful lot of loss. We have experienced a major change in the world and in our personal lives, and this loss must be spoken about. Change often brings loss, and every loss brings change.

I'm sure, like me, you have found that the loss of one thing can mean the gain of another. The loss of a busy lifestyle has given me the gift of time to write. Maybe you have found yourself losing one thing and gaining another, but not necessarily what you thought you'd be dealing with.

In the Bible there is a powerful verse about loss and gain. It says, 'What good is it for someone to gain the whole world yet forfeit their soul.' We have to receive everlasting life, hope, peace, love and a present and future with God, simply by trusting in Jesus.

So, let's bring all our losses to the light, re-evaluate our position, and find a way forward. It's good to be open and honest about the things that have impacted our lives, and to move forward together.

9

COVID BLUES

So how are you feeling? How are you really feeling? Are you, like me, suffering with a mild dose of Covid-19 blues? Nothing too major, but I've been feeling fed up, fatigued and with a dose of fed up-ness. This crisis has gone on for a while now, and it's hard work. That's how I've been feeling. What about you?

It's hardly surprising. We woke up on the morning of the 23rd of March 2020 and our whole world had turned upside down—it was a major life change. We've become more isolated in lockdown, and maybe you are one of the eight million people in the UK who live alone, and that can be really hard at times like these.

Are you missing hugging the people you love and care for? Are you feeling a sense of loss and adjustment? Maybe the only eyes you have gazed into recently are the eyes of the postman delivering that parcel, and that didn't quite nail it for you.

It's really hard, isn't it? We are missing so many things. If you are connected with a church, you will be missing your church family and seeing them face to face. You may be missing your friends, missing your social life, missing your usual activities, and the things that give purpose and structure to your everyday life.

So what can we do about it to lift our spirits? When we look into the Bible, we see a few pointers that will help. When David wrote some of his Psalms he started off by feeling really down, and then he began to lift his eyes to God, to thank God, and praise Him for what he had got rather than focusing on what he hadn't. That might be a good answer for us.

HE IS THE LIFTER OF MY HEAD

We can also fill our hearts and minds with good thoughts, ones that are positive and wholesome. We can read something uplifting and watch good films. We can pursue hobbies and interests, and attempt new recipes that we haven't tackled before, not forgetting there is always chocolate! In all seriousness, when we are down, the only way to go is up.

God is so wonderful at reaching out His hand and lifting us

up when we fall down. If you're not feeling quite on top form today, as I have been recently, you're in good company.

You and I have permission to realise that what we're going through is quite major, and to feel a little bit jaded is to be expected. We all feel the same. We will get through, so lift your head up today. Look to God who can give us the strength we need.

…and then he began to
lift his eyes to God

10

OPPORTUNITY

NEVER LET A GOOD CRISIS GO TO
WASTE. A PESSIMIST SEES THE
DIFFICULTY IN EVERY OPPORTUNITY;
AN OPTIMIST SEES THE
OPPORTUNITY IN EVERY DIFFICULTY.
Winston Churchill

Without doubt, the Covid-19 coronavirus is a global crisis that has impacted, and will continue to impact, millions of lives for a long time. Our world has been turned upside down, but incredible opportunities have also opened up from it as a direct result. The Chinese characters for the word crisis signify both 'danger' and 'opportunity,' so let's give this some consideration:

Fitness – I've seen dogs being walked that haven't seen the light of day for a very long time! (The sort of dog that has not gone much further than their back yard for a while). More walking, more new joggers, and online fitness workouts for kids have been a huge hit.

Innovation – How do we meet when we can't actually meet? How do we do business in lockdown? How do we advertise our product, communicate our encouragement or promote our brand effectively? Technology is such an incredible blessing for us right now. There are so many applications and software for us to use to connect, and this helps the advancing of great projects.

Creativity – We are trying new recipes, decorating our homes, getting our garden landscaped, renovating that old coffee table, fixing that bike, and getting those small chores done that we have put off for a while.

Dreaming – We are not just longing for the day when all this is over and we can get back to a 'new normal', but we are thinking about, planning and dreaming about what we could initiate, or where we can venture one day. We must never stop dreaming.

New things – Have you read a new book? Embarked on learning a new language? Made new friends? Have you discovered a new hobby? Played a new instrument? It's been a time of opportunity for new things.

Slower pace of life – We have been given the gift of time, to rest, relax and replenish. Maybe we needed this more than we realised. Nature needed the rest and maybe we did too.

The Covid-19 pandemic is causing widespread distress and loss. But in it all we can also see great opportunity. Maybe we can discover this for ourselves.

What is the opportunity in this crisis?

11

LONELINESS

I want to ask you a question. Have you ever felt lonely and isolated? I'm sure we all have at different times in our lives, and maybe especially in the Covid-19 crisis. We have perhaps felt lonely and cut off from those we usually do life with, whether that's our family, social group or church, or wherever we feel we belong. Life has looked very different.

Some people live alone, whether by choice or by personal circumstances. It's not necessarily the case that everyone who lives alone is lonely, just as living within a family doesn't make you exempt from feeling alone.

We can all experience loneliness at different times. When on earth, Jesus had times when he felt lonely, and also made a decision to be on his own. He wanted to get away and escape the crowds. (I know that feeling sometimes!)On occasions He was driven out and was rejected. Some people received Christ and welcomed Him, while others rejected Him, just as John says (John 1:11-12). So He would have felt lonely at times. The sense of togetherness came from the group of disciples around Him, with the beautiful like-minded belonging they shared, by walking the same path.

There is a beautiful statement in Psalm 68:6 that helps our loneliness. It says that 'God sets the lonely in families.' Each one of us needs to know that we belong. As a Christian, I'm so happy to belong to God's family. It has given me so many friends in many locations around the world, and we belong together.

Today, I hope and pray that you will feel and know that you belong, and you are safe in God's family. You are safe with those who love you the most.

12

ALL CHANGE

We ventured into 2020 without a care in the world. We had our plans, and our diaries had commitments and appointments in them: holidays we were planning and celebrations we were attending, maybe weddings, birthdays, conferences and overseas travel.

Then one day, on 23rd March, life changed. We were hit with a national crisis with the arrival of the coronavirus pandemic and the need to live life so differently.

All change. Everything changed. Life changed. Plans changed.

Some changes are for the better. The change in the reduction of travel and transport means a notable decrease in air pollution, which seems to have helped nature come alive. The hedgerows are bursting with colour, there are more birds singing than I've heard for a very long time.

I was listening to a documentary about Delhi, India. There, the air there has never been so clear. They have for the first time been able to see the Himalayan Mountains in the far distance.

People seem kinder. Neighbours are reaching out to others around them, even drivers are being more cooperative, and people out walking are greeting each other when, six months ago, they may have just walked by. That might be their main human interaction in their day, so now it has great value.

Life has a different pace now. We have slowed right down. We are doing things in a different way.

We are more grateful than ever for life's simple pleasures of family and home and good food and good weather, and a daily walk has never been so appealing and satisfying.

But not all the changes brought by this crisis are positive. For many there are changes that are hard to process. Let's think of a few:

Loneliness. This crisis is bearable if you live with a family you love in a comfortable home. But if you are alone, you might feel even more isolated. Are there any people living near you who are on their own and need your help? How can you combat your own loneliness? How can you stay in touch with friends and family?

Anxiety. Especially in the early stages of this crisis, where everything was so unsure, there was a huge increase in anxiety levels and that's not surprising. Anxiety is very real, and coupled with depression it can be crippling.

Finances. If you have saved for a rainy day, or are a key worker and still in employment, you may not have experienced financial difficulties. But if you are employed in tourism or the hospitality industry, or on a zero hours contract, or have lost your job in Covid times, this is devastating.

Let's think about all these changes and how they impact us, and those around us. Covid-19 brings change, of that there is no doubt.

13

THE TALE OF TWO APPENDIXES

One Friday night during Covid times, while we were at home, our youngest daughter became very ill and ended up being admitted to hospital by ambulance. Shortly afterwards she had her appendix removed with emergency surgery. It was all quite traumatic and distressing at the time.

This was the day my husband Glen and I were due to be travelling to Canada to visit our eldest daughter and son-in-law, and I was feeling a bit sad that day that we hadn't been able to make the scheduled trip, due to the Covid-19 travel restrictions.

The unusual thing is that, just eight weeks earlier, I, Mum, had had my own appendix removed. How bizarre! I don't think it's catching, is it? These are four things that I've realised since that experience:

1. It was good that we weren't in Canada that weekend as planned, because we needed to be at home. We can't understand life's mysteries or make sense of them, but we needed to be here in Cornwall and not 3,500 miles away. All of us may not be in the place we thought we might be at the moment, because of the Covid crisis, but I was grateful I was where I needed to be.

2. In times of crisis I can never think straight. I can't make even simple decisions. It affects me in that way. But when I couldn't think straight, I still had the capacity to thank. There were so many things I was thanking God for, and now I'm thanking Him that He brought our daughter safely home so I could nurse her in the comfort of our family home. So when I can't think, I can always thank.

3. I can fully empathise with my daughter during her recovery because I have walked that path before her. Every little ailment and concern, I can help with—not just sympathise but totally empathise, from personal experience.

It made me think about Jesus, coming from heaven to earth so that He could absolutely empathise with humanity: to feel how we really feel. Hebrews 4:15 says, 'We do not have a high priest who is unable to empathise with our weaknesses', because He is God who took on human form, in order to be our Saviour. He is 'God with us' and we are never left on our own.

4. When we saw our daughter leave in the ambulance, and we couldn't be with her, it was a massive comfort to this mother's heart
that God was with her. Some of us may be separated right now from our loved ones during this crisis. We've got a big gap between us and those we love, but we know that God fills that gap. He fills our hearts with hope and love and peace, and we know that, in everything, God is with us. He's promised never to leave us nor forsake us.

14

HOPE DEFERRED

My 2020 diary looks empty. There are so many things cancelled, rescheduled, completely done away with, or being done in a different way. Items have been removed that are no longer relevant to this season that we're in.

There were things in my diary I was really looking forward to, and had set my hopes on, only to have those hopes dashed.

Solomon, when writing the book of Proverbs, sums up how we might feel. He says in Proverbs 13:12 that 'hope deferred makes the heart sick.' When we hope for, have an expectation of, and set our sights on something and it can't happen, we feel deflated.

The word 'sick' means to feel grieved and sad. When things don't happen as we thought they might, we can feel disappointed, and psychologists tell us that disappointment can trigger feelings of depression. What we need to remember at this time is that we have our hope deferred. What we had longed for can't happen quite yet, but can happen and it will happen one day, all being well. It's just that it can't happen right now.

So once we understand why we sometimes feel a bit down, it is easier to accept. We know that storms don't last forever and there are better days ahead for us. We know that we may have been robbed of many things over the weeks and months, but we haven't been stripped of everything.

There were some things that were really important to us, but we have not been denied them ever happening; they are just not going to happen quite yet. There's a delay, and that's the difference. That gives us the strength and the hope to keep pressing on. We've got to go one day at a time. It can't happen now, but it may happen soon.

15

GERANIUM

I want to show you this beautiful geranium plant in my garden that is looking absolutely spectacular. As I've been looking at this plant while I've been sitting outdoors, I've seen a lesson that I want to pass on to you, to inspire and encourage.

This plant reminds me that our lives have seasons, cycles, chapters and verses. I see the flowers that have flourished and have now fallen away. They are making room for new things. Life is like that sometimes. We have to let go of something in order to embrace the new, and that includes loss and change and adjustment, and we should never be afraid of that.

Then I see the flowers that are blossoming. They're not pretending to be a petunia or a daisy; they're just being geranium. They are being just who God made them to be. There is something inherently beautiful in their just being who they are.

Maybe there's a lesson there for us as well: just bloom and blossom and be who we are, shining just the way we are without comparing ourselves to others.

Then, as we look a bit more closely at this plant, we see there is so much potential in the new buds. I don't think we realise the potential that's within each one of us, too. There is such potential that is yet to blossom and unfold and unfurl.

So my prayer for you today is that you would understand the seasons and cycles of life.

DON'T FEAR LOSS, CHANGE, AND LETTING GO.

BE YOU AND SHINE.

REALISE YOUR POTENTIAL.

16

PSALM 23
THE SHEPHERD

We have a small flock of sheep, and when my husband, Glen, calls them, they go running to him. I do not have that superpower, but my husband certainly does. They know that he is their shepherd and they trust him. He calls them and they go to him. It is the most beautiful sight to see.

And so it is with our Good Shepherd: He leads, guides us, protects us and provides for us. He calls us by our name and we are really safe when we follow Him.

Every good leader/shepherd can be followed. Sometimes the journey takes us beside the 'still and quiet waters' where all is calm. At other times, we go through the 'valley of the shadow of death.' That is a different path – it's dangerous, uncertain and there is a shadow cast over our lives, just like in Covid times.

For these times we see the Shepherd with His rod and staff.

The staff or shepherd's crook will draw us close when we might be prone to wander.

In His other hand is the rod, with which the Shepherd fights off all the things that come against the sheep. In the literal setting it would have been the wild animals that roar loudly. For us, metaphorically, it is the roar of negativity, weariness and hopelessness. Our Good Shepherd can be trusted.

When Jesus called the disciples at the start of the Gospels, He simply said to them, 'Follow me.' There was no small print, no contract, and no detail of what that life would mean. It was simply a call to take a step of faith that said, 'I will follow you, and I know that I can trust you wherever you go.'

I hope that settles in your heart and gives you peace today. You have a Shepherd, and He cares for His sheep.

17

PSALM 23
THE RESTORED SOUL

I occasionally venture to the depths of my husband's workshop and garage. I have to be careful not to touch anything or move anything, because he knows where everything is and if anything was misplaced, he would know!

It's where he mends and restores things, and is so clever doing so. Glen recently restored some dining chairs belonging to friends and fixed them up. They had gone a bit rickety and he mended them, and they are as good as new. Isn't it wonderful when something that was broken gets restored, refurbished and is given a new future? Surely that's what restoration is all about.

Psalm 23, possibly the best-known psalm of all, says, 'The Lord...restores my soul' (NKJ version). I'm so glad He has done that, and is continuing to do that for me. I think the clue to the restoration is found in the previous verses, that say, 'The Lord is my Shepherd... He makes me lie down in green pastures, He leads me beside quiet waters.' Then it says, 'He restores my soul.' Could it be that at this time of enforced rest during the Covid-19 pandemic, there is an opportunity for restoration? Our usual pace of life has changed, and rest certainly aids restoration.

Everything does seem to be coming alive again. What if you and I are coming alive again? What if, in times of rest, God is restoring our soul, because everything is restored for a future use. God has a great future ahead for each one of us as we put our trust, hope and our confidence in Him.

David knew what it was like to be restored. Previously, after an experience of failure, he had written Psalm 51, that says, 'Create in me a pure heart, O God, and renew a steadfast spirit within me. Do not cast me from your presence or take your Holy Spirit from me. *Restore* to me the joy of your salvation.' He can take our brokenness, fix us up and give us hope and a future. It is what God does.

Truth told in Covid times

18

PSALM 23
THE SMALL FLOCK

I'm talking about sheep again, not just because I'm a Welsh girl and there are reputedly eleven million sheep in Wales! That's not the reason. As a family, we have a flock of sheep on some land that we rent, very close to where we live. There are currently twenty-one of them – my husband counts them each day!

The story began six years ago, when our daughter Bethany had six sheep for Christmas. They were a bit difficult to gift wrap – let me tell you!

Today, our daughter and her husband make their home in Canada, and she is employed by a large sheep farm, now looking after a flock of 4,500 sheep! She started with just six, and there is a beautiful thing that I see in this story.

We must be faithful with the small things, the seemingly insignificant, and watch things grow - greater, bigger, broader and deeper.

The Bible says to never despise the day of small things and so many times we see this portrayed for us in its pages – just think about Jesus' parable of the mustard seed and the feeding of the five thousand with five loaves and two small fish, to name a couple.

So what is in your hand that you think is small? You might say, 'It's only a little something I can contribute. It's only a little something that I do.' Don't despise it.

What small people are in your world? Your children or those you love and care for, and are looking after. It might be a small project that you're working on, a small craft business that you have just set up, or a small church that you are part of, or a small group that you are part of.

It may not be big, but small things can have a big impact, as I recall when I needed to have my appendix removed during Covid times. In Luke's Gospel, Jesus teaches that when we are faithful with small things we will also be faithful in greater things and in more things.

So I'm challenging you today to not despise the day of small things that you're involved with, because watch what can happen when you are faithful in the small. God will take care of the rest. What a journey it was to go from six to four thousand five hundred sheep, but it simply began one sheep at a time, one step at a time and everything else will follow on. In these Covid times, what is in our hand may seem small at the moment, but watch this space!

What is in your hand?

19

PSALM 23
FACING FEAR

Are you afraid of the dark or of spiders, or of deep water or maybe bats and flying creatures? Or possibly, like me, might you be afraid of the dentist? I'm not consumed with fear, I just don't like it much. It is a completely irrational fear. Every time I've been to the dentist and had a checkup or some treatment, when I drive home I always think to myself, 'Oh, that wasn't so bad.' I remind myself that my fear wasn't rational.

Fear is a very real emotion and it can grip us sometimes and make us feel very uncomfortable. During the Covid-19 crisis I have seen so much fear. We've all experienced some measure of fear because everything is so unknown. We watch the media, and we look in our newspapers, and we hear things, we see other people's fears stirred up, and it affects us.

In our garden two years ago we had a lovely crop of

raspberries, but last year something sad happened. A plant called 'bindweed' began to attach itself to the raspberry canes. It's got a beautiful white, bell-like flower and is very common in the summer, but the stalks wrap themselves around other plants and choke them. So much so that our raspberry canes are no more.

They were overcome by this bindweed that took a grip on the plant, and the whole lot has been destroyed. Fear is very much like that! Last summer I remember talking to the bindweed and saying, 'How dare you do this to my raspberries!' (I hope no neighbours were listening). How dare fear try and encroach on our lives, too, and cripple us so that we never venture out of our comfort zone.

On a personal level, I've needed to conquer fear recently, in connection with my website, my video 'thought for the day' and my written material.

I've needed to overcome the fear of 'What if it fails? What if nobody watches? What if nobody reads what I ever put into print? What if they think it is rubbish? What if they think I'm trying to set up myself to be something that I'm not?'

These are very real fears and I have had to say that I am going to put those fears to one side and I am going to press on. This is God's time, and if I can bring some encouragement to people, then I want to do this. It is God's word, and that never returns to him empty (Isaiah 55:11). When we plant a seed, God takes responsibility for the rest of the process. All we need to do is plant it, and see it grow. So I've tried to deal with my fears for this Truth Told project that I'm working on.

SOMETIMES OUR FEARS ARE RATIONAL AND SOMETIMES THEY'RE NOT.

Fear is real, but each one of us can conquer and overcome it. God's word says that 'perfect love drives out all fear.'

Psalm 23 says, 'I will fear no evil, for You are with me.' That's the solution for dealing with our fear. 'You are with me'. God is with me, dealing with my fear. He promised to never leave me or forsake me.

If someone comes with me to the dentist's and sits in the waiting room with me - that will alleviate my fears. We chat about other things and it takes my mind off it. Someone is with me.

How much more is our ever-present Heavenly Father with us every step of the way! Take your fears to God and know His peace.

I WILL FEAR NO EVIL
FOR *YOU* ARE WITH ME

RELEVANT BIBLE VERSES
IN THE BOOK:

PSALM 23
A PSALM OF DAVID

1 The LORD is my shepherd, I lack nothing.

2 He makes me lie down in green pastures, he leads me beside quiet waters,

3 he refreshes my soul. He guides me along the right paths for his name's sake.

4 Even though I walk through the darkest valley, I will fear no evil, for you are with me; your rod and your staff, they comfort me.

5 You prepare a table before me in the presence of my enemies. You anoint my head with oil; my cup overflows.

6 Surely goodness and love will follow me all the days of my life, and I will dwell in the house of the LORD forever

COVID 19 OBSERVATIONS FROM SOME OF SARAH'S FRIENDS:

In Covid times I learnt how precious my family is, and it almost hurt that we couldn't hug for weeks/months. I learnt also that I have very kind neighbours and made new connections walking a neighbour's dog regularly, as they were unable to go out, which meant a lot to both of us.

***

Covid lockdown for us as a family has meant inclusion. As a family with a teen with special needs, it is often hard to get to events, and suddenly everyone was in the same boat. We recognise it has been a hard, grief-filled time for some, but for us (and many other special needs families) it has been a time of inclusion.

***

I have been reminded above all of God's faithfulness, that when I seek Him in that secret place, He restores my soul—over and over again. Whatever the future holds, 'It is well with my soul.' I have also learned that when we see the human family through God's eyes, from His perspective, we are all precious in His sight.

***

I learned to live in the moment and not take anything for granted.

It's best not to buy ten pairs of shoes online, only to discover that the shop won't be reopening so they can't be taken back!

***

In Covid times I learnt to explore my local area, to find an unexplored path and walk it. I really enjoyed my 'lockdown walks'. I love my cat, Jasper, but learnt how much company and mental well-being he provides me, and that he makes a good working from home friend.

***

I've been reflecting on what's essential and what's not. Essentials are family, friends, colleagues and faith. I've seen a deepening of personal relationships and less worrying about material things. The most used new phrase is 'You're on mute.'

***

In Covid times I learnt that it's OK to enjoy a slower pace of life and enjoy things you wouldn't normally have time for, such as gardening, watching wildlife in the garden and spending less time in front of the TV in the evenings! In Covid times I felt fortunate to live near my family and friends and be able to see them from a distance when times were hard.

***

In Covid times I learned...the value of connection. Finding new ways to connect when we are not able to see each other; using technology enabled me to reach out and connect with people both near and far.

I learnt the value of home, family and friendships and reaching out to those who need a helping hand. I feel we are all in this together. Being united in this fight brought moments of amazing kindness and many highs and lows.

**

In Covid times I learnt that I am enough. Being a single mum, I have always chased around meeting friends, going on playdates and taking my son to all sorts of events. At the start of lockdown we couldn't leave the house apart from work and nursery. Luckily we have a large garden so my son and I spent precious time together, making mud pies in the garden, and painting rocks. I realised I am enough for him, he had a great time, and despite it being quite stressful at times with missing the rest of the family, so did I.

**

In Covid times I learnt what's most important in life and to me.

**

I've learnt that you don't appreciate what you've got until you don't have it, and sometimes the simplest things in life give the most pleasure.

**

A smile from a stranger whilst out shopping is a wonderful thing.

In Covid times I have also learned that when having online meetings with your camera on, to remember to make sure your bra isn't hanging on the radiator behind you!

***

In Covid times I learned how to persevere, even if it felt like the world was closing in on me. I just finished college yesterday, at the age of 55. I never thought I would have the opportunity to go to college; now I have had to complete it alone, at home, only having once a day Zoom chats with my teacher. God is so good!

***

I have learnt that baking is not such a mystery after all.

***

In Covid times I learnt to simplify my life, pause and realise relationships are the most important thing. It's been freeing to see we can do ministry differently in ways we wouldn't have thought of before.

***

In Covid times I've learned to... S.L.O.W. D.O.W.N!!!!

***

I've learned to be patient, to slow down and open my eyes to what I've missed through the rush of life and breathe in the goodness of God.

In Covid times I learned to be totally reliant on God's grace in every part of my life.

***

I have realised that we do not need half the stuff that we would normally buy when not in lockdown. Let us praise the Lord for what He supplies and learn to pray for guidance to spend more wisely.

***

Don't take things for granted. Even something as simple as a hug is priceless. I missed this the most.

***

I've learnt that you really need your mum around when you've had a lockdown baby!

***

In Covid times I learnt that almost everyone recognises that they have a duty to each other and to society as a whole, and that we are capable of astounding demonstrations of care and appreciation of each other. This was a great help in dealing with my Dad's death from Covid, when the support I would usually have given in person to my step-Mum was not possible. It was lovely to know that there were so many others tenderly wrapping their (virtual) arms around her.

In COVID times I learned that life is actually simpler than what we've made it - Love God - Love family. Love life itself.

In Covid times I learned to appreciate the things that for so long I had taken for granted. I also learnt perspective. That some of the things I thought were important, really aren't, but that connection with other people was a lot more important than previously thought, and I will never take for granted ever again having people around me, especially those that mean a lot to me. Covid times have been good for me. I'm not sure grateful is the right word but I'm not sad that Covid happened, to me anyway (I obviously wouldn't wish this on others as I am fully aware of the devastation this pandemic has brought on others).

***

In Covid times I have learnt that my own company is OK.

***

That family is very precious. That I don't need to buy any more clothes for the rest of my life (well, almost!). That I have too many things in my diary (I have now dropped a couple of things). That I enjoy waking up at 6.15am and having time with God and reading and not feeling pressured to get up and be somewhere every day. That I can start and finish a project - I've made a patchwork quilt and am enjoying painting!

WHAT DID YOU LEARN IN COVID TIMES?

PHOTO CREDITS:

- Unexpected place - Belinda Fewings on Unsplash
- Being and doing - Sarah Chaplin
- Hold tight - Sarah Chaplin
- Best and worst - Tim Mossholder on Unsplash
- Worry - Boram Kim on Unsplash
- Keep running - Adi Goldstein on Unsplash
- Darkness - Bernard Tuck on Unsplash
- Loss - Rebekah Chaplin
- Covid blues - Ben White on Unsplash
- Opportunity - Paul Skorupskas on Unsplash
- Loneliness - Rebekah Chaplin
- All change - Ross Findon on Unsplash
- Appendix - D.R. on Unsplash
- Hope deferred - Aron Visuals on Unsplash
- Geranium - Sarah Chaplin
- Shepherd - Sarah Chaplin
- Restored soul - K.B on Unsplash
- Small flock - Caleb Lucas on Unsplash
- Fear - Sarah Chaplin

ABOUT THE AUTHOR

Sarah Chaplin is an inspirational speaker and author and the founder of Truth Told, and loves communicating truth.

Sarah was born in South Wales, and is married to Glen, with four young adult children and a wonderful son-in-law. They make their home in Cornwall, UK. Having been born without a left hand, Sarah has a great story which has inspired many people through the years. Brought up in a family who had personal faith in God, at the age of twelve in Sunday School, Sarah discovered this faith for herself, and has never looked back.

In the late 1990s Glen and Sarah spent two years working in Zambia at a Bible College and Agricultural Project, and continue to have a passion for Missions, with Glen now working for Harvesters Ministries (www.harvestersministries.com) having served as a church pastor for twenty years.

Sarah regularly speaks and shares her 'Singlehanded' story at events and conferences in different locations around the UK and further afield, and loves to communicate the truth of God's Word in an inspirational, relevant and practical way.

Currently working as a part-time hospital chaplain at an acute regional hospital in Cornwall, Sarah is also a great lover of music, particularly playing the keyboard and singing, and loves travelling, spending time with friends, and making new ones.

ACKNOWLEDGMENTS

With heartfelt thanks to Phyl Morgan, entrepreneur, investor and pastor and, more importantly, close friend of Glen and me. Phyl was instrumental in the setting up of my website and has encouraged me to 'get out there and communicate truth' at this time. I'm so grateful.

I'm indebted to David Matthew, my editor and the one who gives such helpful advice. Former teacher, Bible School lecturer, church leader and author of many books himself, his fatherly encouragement and wisdom have been invaluable.

To my wonderful husband, Glen and our four young adult children, Joshua, Bethany (and her husband Josh), Rebekah and Benjamin, for their love and support for me, and for *Truth Told*.

www.truthtold.org.uk

https://www.facebook.com/truthtoldUK

COMING SOON

PEARLS FOR THE GIRLS is a coffee-table type book with inspired illustrations as a project with my friend Melanie Chadwick, a freelance illustrator and designer living and working in Cornwall. Her work is on her website: www.melaniechadwick.com

'I am delighted to commend this book to you. In it you will get to meet the real Sarah. She writes as she is, full of honesty and humour. I have been trying to encourage Sarah to put it together for a long time, as it seemed obvious to me that her pearls of wisdom needed to be shared with others. It is also clear that this book will be useful in many different contexts. Sarah is an amazing woman, full of rich wisdom and abundant love for others. She has an incredible gift of communicating, which is demonstrated in these pages and in beautiful collaboration with Mel's inspired artwork and encouragement for personal application.'
Dr Tamie Downes - Oxford